HOW TO GET OUT OF THE

"UNFULFILLING" RELATIONSHIP

for Single Women

From a Biblical/Christian

perspective

Tara Phillips, MS, MSW, LCSW

Unless otherwise indicated, all Scriptural references are taken from the King James Version (KJV) of the Holy Bible. This author gives all literary credit to the Holy Spirit.

DISCLAIMER

This book is designed to provide information only. This book is not for women actively in a physically abusive or otherwise dangerous relationship. If you are in this situation get immediate assistance from law enforcement. This information is provided and sold with the knowledge that the publisher and author do not offer any legal advice. This book also does not contain all the information available on the subject. Every effort has been made to make this book as accurate as possible. This book should serve as a general guide and not as the ultimate source of subject information. The author and publisher shall have no liability or responsibility to any person or entity regarding any damage incurred directly or indirectly, by the information contained in this book.

Book Review

"This guide was truly enlightening and as a single woman, very, very relevant. The reading quickly delved into the business of defining an unfulfilling relationship as well as communicating specific steps for letting go. I found myself quickly engaged and felt comforted by the examples and narrative included. Most important for me were the multiple opportunities for self-reflection offered throughout the guide. I even found myself laughing out loud as I answered some of the questions about myself. Kudos to this author, who left me with renewed confidence in my own ability to establish a fulfilling relationship. The author does identify a target population, but this guide is certainly chock-full of wisdom about relationships and spirituality that anyone can gain from."

Clarissa A. Lewis, Licensed Professional Counselor

Dedication

This book is dedicated to my mother, Janie Parks, who is so precious to me. I love you mama! It is also dedicated to my children Paige, Holly, Christian and Kennedy, who needed to see their mother finally finish something!

Contents

INTRODUCTION

Hi, thank you for taking the time to pick up this book. It was birthed to help someone. It may help you or another woman that you love. It is also designed to help young teenage girls who are entering adulthood. Now for the teenagers, I recommend that a parent or trusted adult read it along with them. This book is intended for single women. This is not a book for married women on how to get out of a relationship. Although many women are divorced, this book is not an advocate for divorce. This book is for women who are single and are in an unfulfilling relationship. Or for single women who want to have a more fulfilling relationship in the future.

Also, this book is not a male bashing book. The author loves men and knows that we need them. There are many wonderful men in the world. While the book addresses an unfulfilling relationship, it will focus on some characteristics of males as they relate to them being in a relationship with a woman. But this book is ultimately for women.

Also, if you are a woman in a crisis situation, such as an abusive relationship, this book is not for you right now. Your first order of business is to get to safety. Tell someone you trust, get law enforcement involved and get to safety, don't play around with your life. There are many victims of domestic violence each year who are no longer with us. Once you are in a safe place, by all means read this book as it will help you heal and prepare your heart in the future for a new relationship.

As the author, I am a divorced mother myself and have experienced my share of unfulfilling relationships. I am a work in progress. So I have lived through this book personally. As the old saying goes, "I am practicing what I'm preaching". I have a heart for women, we go through so much in life. If any part of my life can help others I want to be that help. I hope you enjoy this book. If this book helps you in anyway please reach out to me at www.taraphillipsconsulting.com. I look forward to hearing from you. I am a Christian Counselor for women. I write and present workshops for women from a Biblical/Christian perspective and I consult businesses on how to improve and retain their client relationships.

What do most unfulfilling relationships look like?

You don't hear from him daily like you would like. You call him, but you don't get an answer. You figure he must be busy and he'll call you back. So you leave him a message or you text him. "Hi sweetie thinking about you". Hours go by no return call, no text. Your mind starts to wander does he really love me? Is there someone else? You reluctantly call back, still no answer. Now you can't think about much else. You still have two more hours at work, but you can't focus. You rationalize I know he's probably just busy. I'm making too much of this. You muddle through work. Your co-worker tries to make conversation with you but you're not interested in talking to her. You get a text, your face lights up as you check your phone. It's not him, it's a friend sending an inspirational text. You wish she wouldn't send those especially when you're waiting on a text or phone call from your guy. About 10 minutes before work ends, your phone rings. It's him. You're beaming from ear to ear. You scurry to a quiet spot to talk.

"Hey babe, I've been missing you".

"I miss you too" he replies.

"Are we still going to see that movie later?" you ask.

"Yeah, I'm going over to my mother's house, she's cooking for me. We can go after that, oh babe I gotta go, I gotta another call", he says.

"Bye", you say. You are a little baffled because you two had plans before the movie. But oh well, it's okay you will see him later.

You go home and clean up, eat dinner alone and get ready for your date. By 9pm, you start to get concerned, no phone call or texts from him on his whereabouts. You call and he answers with no concern in his voice, you hear others in the background laughing.
"Are you coming? you ask.

"Oooh, I forgot I'm over here with my family, I forgot can we go another day?" he asks.

"Sure, but you don't treat me like a priority in your life", you say tiredly.

"Oh babe, don't start this I'm here having a good time with my family I told you we will go another day" he says.

"Whatever", you say and hang up.

This same scenario with different variations has happened several times in the past few months that you have been dating him. He knows you like to communicate daily. It doesn't have to be long conversation but just to say hello and for you to know how his day is going and vice versa. The more you say what you need from the relationship the less you receive it. When you call him, if he answers, you feel as if you have invaded his space. When he calls you, you drop everything and give him your full attention. This occurs about 2-3 times per week. All of your plans for your future include him or you want him included. You think about him when you wake up and when you lie down to go to sleep. When he does spend time with you, you feel like you hit the lottery.

When you do spend more than a few hours with him it's for sex when he wants it. It wasn't obvious at first, but it is now. But you take whatever time you can get with him because he tells you he is busy, on the grind, working hard. You are not happy with this relationship, but you love him. You don't know how to make him love you, how you need him to. You don't know how to make him see you and really miss you when you're away. You don't know how to get him to spend more time with you. But most importantly, you don't know how to leave him alone.

If any of this is familiar, put on your seatbelt this ride is for you. Many of our relationships follow this fashion in some form or the other. There are many different variations of the same theme. But always the same bottom line remains......I'm not getting the love I deserve. Unfulfilling relationships can have many different components that make them unfulfilling such as cheating, distrust, lack of communication, not enough quality time and several other factors. For the purposes of this book when I discuss our male counterpart his name will be "Joe". This name is short and simple and has no direct reference to anyone in particular. This book is not about Joe it's about you, us or women in general.

How We Love

As women we love hard, we know exactly what that means. Women are natural comforters, nurturers and bonders. Most of us seek to have one person with whom to have a monogamous loving relationship. Sounds so simple to us. We not only provide love, we provide support and we have your back in any situation. There is hardly a limit to what we won't do when we show our love. So, why does it seem to come back to us void? We take it personal when we don't get at least an attempt of the same type of love back to us. Loving is easy for us. It's a part of our DNA. But just as much as we have the propensity to give love, we want and need love to be returned to us as well.

Many times as women we confuse love with "words of love". Lots of men are skilled in speaking "words of love" for example, "You are beautiful", "You are the only one I want", "I could spend the rest of my life with you", "You know I love you, girl", "I don't need anybody but you", "You are the best thing that's happened to me", "I would never cheat on you" "I love being with you", "You are the only one for me". Joe knows that these words work to get you interested. Unfortunately, most of these words will not be backed up by his actions. As women, we want to believe Joe's words, the problem is, we believe the words without seeing the evidence or actions that should correspond with the words.

Unfortunately, as women, if we don't grow up with a positive male role model in our lives we don't have an opportunity to know what a great man should sound like or act like. We lack a standard of comparison. As women we are verbal communicators, so when Joe "says the right things" we believe he will "do the right things".

Why do we love like this?

I have two theories based upon biblical principles on why women can experience the intensity of love or the need for love so greatly. As Adam and Eve were being led out of the Garden of Eden, God pronounced their punishment for failing to follow his commands. Eve's curse was:

Genesis 3:16

"Unto the woman, he said, I will greatly multiply thy sorrow and they conception; in sorrow thou shalt bring forth children; **and thy desire shall be to thy husband**, and he shall rule over thee."

Wow! Under the curse, we will run after a man to try to make him love us. This is a curse that many young women unknowingly agree with by their actions. Many young women today have not had a positive male role models in their lives. There is no father that sets the standard on how their daughters engage in communication with the opposite sex. These young women pursue men in an effort to have a male in their lives who loves them. What they really need is unconditional love, which is definitely not what they will receive from their pursuits. They run after Joe so hard that Joe doesn't have a desire or even need to pursue them. Joe simply has to decide how to juggle the opportunities presented to him. He typically won't just choose one, but he will instead put them in rotation. Joe will have several relationships that are fulfilling to him, but are unfulfilling to the women. Joe will become a liar because he can't keep his word to everyone, therefore he doesn't keep his word to anyone.

Conventional wisdom has taught us as women to be proactive and if we see a man that we want we can be the aggressor. We can pursue him. Whether or not you agree with this philosophy, one thing is true as women we need Joe to continuously tell us he loves us in some fashion or another. If you have pursued Joe, you will always wonder if he really wants you. So therefore you will always question his love for you. And if Joe is not a great man he will just be satisfied and remember you came after him, so he has no need to work for something that was given to him.

Genesis 2:23-24

"And Adam said, This is now bone of my bones and flesh of my flesh: she shall be called Woman, because she was taken out of Man.

Therefore shall a man leave his father and his mother, and shall cleave unto his wife; and they shall be one flesh".

Couples when they marry and consummate the marriage become one flesh.

Sex outside of marriage: What's the big deal?

But what happens when two people who are not married have sex? Sex causes connection and is another level of intimacy. In the bible when sex is mentioned it is in reference to people "knowing each other" such as "And Adam knew Eve his wife; and she conceived, and bare Cain………" (Genesis 4:1). This connection of the physical body with another's is a gift from God for two people in a marriage. So, sex in biblical terms is a gift that gives pleasure to a husband and wife. It is one way they express love to each other. Sex is also a way to increase or maintain a stable population. We all are the product of sex, except for interesting advancements in science that we've heard about. It is not something to be taken lightly as you will see.

From the world's viewpoint, sex is defined as an act with at least two people. They don't have to be married. Sex has been reduced to another activity of dating. No level of commitment is required. It's just something you do after a magical number of dates or even the first. Sex is a tool that is used to encourage another to be in a relationship with you. Sex is another form of entertainment. We have dinner and see a movie and sex is just another event of the evening. Most believe that Joe can have sex with anyone, it's just an act, and he doesn't have to care about or love that person. It's like riding a bicycle or tying shoe laces. The results of sex is euphoric for somebody. For Joe, it's great, he had fun. For you it may be great and fun, but as women, we expect a greater connection with you. Usually, the relationship before and after sex is unsatisfying with Joe anyway. Sex may be used as a way to get him to be more committed. Sex may be a way to make sure you steal his heart away from another. Sex never gets you what you really want does it? You really want his heart and his love. Sex becomes a weapon, a tool, part of an arsenal of war. It doesn't sound like fun anymore does it? So what happens when two or more people who are not married have sex?

Two single people having sex don't become one flesh as in marriage. But their souls become entangled. This entanglement allows what occurs in one person's life to have access and flow into the other person's life. This transfer doesn't discriminate and will always be negative. If sex is a gift for married couples given by God. So when sex is taken or stolen by single people it becomes a curse. Wow! That extracurricular activity no longer seems so insignificant does it? Let's talk a little about Joe. He doesn't communicate with you as well as you would like him to. Also, you realize that in your conversations with him, that he doesn't share much. You realize that you do most of the talking.You really don't know much about Joe other than surface topics. He gives you the compliments "words of love" we mentioned earlier. But something is missing, you don't know who Joe really is nor does he share other parts of his life with you. He shows up when he wants to, not necessarily when you need him. So you are left alone most of the time, waiting and looking forward to your next communication with him. You need him to give you his time, which he rations out to you like an occasional dessert.You hope he is not, but it crosses your mind that he may be seeing someone else.

You and Joe have sex when you spend time together. It's not necessarily enjoyable on its own but it pleases you to be in his space. And it seems to please him a lot. So your soul is entangled with Joe's. Now what if Joe is having sex with not only you but "Jane" as well. That means, if Jane has a disease, she can give it to Joe. Then unfortunately, Joe can share it with you. You and Jane don't know each other but now, physically she has affected your health. The same is true spiritually for other issues. Whatever occurs in the life of Joe or Jane now has access to your life and vice versa. If either has issues of depression, suicide, poverty, grief, loss, strife, anger, etc. You have now given these issues an open door into your life. This is part of the spiritual manifestation that sex can bring into the life of those not married to each other. Also, as you add more people the whole scenario gets to be sickening physically and spiritually. Another major error is when you think that your actions only affect you. When you as a single woman have sex with Joe, not only do you open up your life to him and anyone else he is intimate with, but woe if you have children!!!! You have now opened up their innocent lives to the consequences of your sin.

How do I come out?

I love him! Why doesn't time heal all wounds? Why doesn't this relationship work, I am doing all that I can.

"What I need (to be emotionally healthy) is more important than what I want"   T. Phillips, 2013

You must first want to come out of the relationship. For a lot of women this unfulfilling relationship is enough for them. There standards for Joes are low anyway. Which in turn means, their standards for themselves are even lower. They have no expectations of anything better. Some of them are so accustomed to being ignored, neglected and cheated on that it's no big deal. First, you must identify that the relationship is unhealthy. Still some decide that a bad relationship is better than no relationship at all. That's like saying a moldy bag of bread, is still useful, just wipe off the mold. Many women struggle with what they saw growing up. If mom was in a bad relationship and it worked or appeared to work for her, why should I expect any better? What does this mean for you? Although you want the relationship with him, it is not what you need. What do you need? You need love. You think you know how to love. You realize that the same love you are willing to give is not being given back to you. The relationship feels one-sided, lop-sided, unbalanced and unequal. So what do you do? Breakup and start and new relationship with someone else? Is that the issue? Or is there more involved? There is much more involved. The change doesn't need to occur in him, it needs to occur in you. What! I'm not the unloving person, I'm not the one neglecting the relationship! Or are you? Laziness is not just on Joe's part. "If you want something different you have to do something different". " If you want things to be different you have to become something different".

You come out by learning the true order of love. When you get it you will become an unstoppable force and able to leap tall, cute, and no good Joe's with a single bound.

The True Order of Love

Exodus 20:3 "Thou shalt have no other gods before me"

Am I suggesting that you may be treating Joe like a god? Yes, I am. Do you think about him when you get up in the morning? Do you think about him before you go to bed at night? Do you worry about talking to him during the day? Do you get excited when you talk to him? Do you enjoy spending time with him? Now, if you had a choice to spend time with Joe or God, which would you choose?

Uh-oh! Guess what? During the times when Joe is not showing you love or spending time with you? Are you sad? Do you miss him?

What if I told you God has been missing you, like you miss Joe? Also, do you realize that you are getting what you give to God? Luke 6:38 talks about the law of giving. Joe is actually following God's law and doesn't even know it. He spends time with you like you spend time with God. Your relationship with God determines everything in your life. If you don't have a relationship with God, your life is a mess. This is certain.

Now how often do you spend time with God? Although, we can't see him, God is there all the time. When Joe doesn't show up, God is there. When Joe doesn't call, God is there. When you are sad and lonely, God is there. The issue you have with Joe is that he may say that he loves you, but he doesn't have actions to back up his words. God is love.

Is any of this true for you? You don't spend enough time with God. God is not your priority. You don't think about God in the morning or before you go to sleep. You don't call on God, until you need something. You don't talk to God everyday. God desires your presence daily, but you don't give it to Him. If God spoke with you about your relationship with Him, would He say you spend enough time with Him? Would he say that He felt close to you? Would He want you to spend more time with Him? Do you get excited to spend time with Him?

Okay, take a breath, don't get mad please keep reading. So all that being said, God should be your first love. Why? Because He said so and if you are out of order with Him, how do you expect other things in your life to go well? Putting God first has amazing repercussions on your life. Let me show you what it does. Whatever we honor first determines how successful we are in life. The world would tell us to "Put yourself first". It might sound cute, but it's a desperately flawed secular view. This consequence not only affects the relationships of regular people, its laws affects the relationships of those who are famous as well. If you watch a public famous relationship that doesn't follow this order eventually it will end. Unfortunately, because it is public you are able to see what's going on behind the scenes. My heart goes out to all women who suffer in relationships, especially those in the public eye, because they are not allowed the anonymity and time to heal.

How do I put God first?

A. Reading God's word

One of the best ways to put God first, is to spend time reading His word. You could decide to do this the first thing in the morning. Your mind hopefully at this time will be refreshed and renewed from sleep. If you have spent time reading the word before, you will know what to do. If not, that's okay. While the whole bible, Old and New Testament should be read, a good place to start as you are reading this book is the book of Matthew. It discusses the genealogy of Jesus Christ and His life. It speaks of God's love for his people. As the entire bible ultimately focuses on Jesus Christ, it would be a good place to begin your reading. Many scholars and philosophers have opinions about how to read the bible and how to read all of the bible in a certain period of time. All I want you to focus on is reading one chapter per day. If you have a desire to read more please do so, but the one chapter a day will be very beneficial to you. If you can put your hands on a study bible that will be even better as it will have a summary about the meaning of what you are reading. Everyone that is a reader of the word has different approaches to how they go about this. You will have to develop your own. I don't read just to read but I try to read for comprehension, when I don't understand a portion, find the meaning. There are some trusted resources available on the internet. I personally will read a portion of the Old and New Testament daily and the next day I keep going forward where I left off the day before. Also, there are many versions of the bible, check them out on the internet and see which version is best for you. As you will notice the different versions can help with your comprehension.

B. Prayer

Spending time in prayer to God is another great way to put Him first. If you have not been spending time with Him and don't know what to say, tell Him that. You could say: "Father, I know I have not been spending time with you, please forgive me for my sins (be specific about what they are), I want to love you more than anyone or anything else in this world teach me how in Jesus' name I pray. Amen"

This is a great prayer, you have to start somewhere. As you begin to read the Word and pray this simple prayer, God will begin shining in your heart and your prayers will change and you will become closer to God. You find God in His word. As women, we have many feeling and emotions. But believing God's word is not about our feelings, but if we first believe His word He will create "right" feelings within us. If you can take the stance that all God's word is true, you will automatically increase your faith.

If we allow God to be our first love…………

"I love them that love me; and those that seek me early shall find me". (Proverbs 8:17)

*He will change you from the inside out (you are new) "Therefore if any man be in Christ, he is a new creature: old things are passed away behold, all things are become new". (2 Cor 5:17)

*He will tell you who you are (He will name you) "But as many as received him, to them gave He power to become the sons (and daughters) of God, even to them that believe on His name. (John 1:12).

*We accept the love He first showed to us "For God so loved the world that He gave His only begotten Son, that whosoever believeth in Him should not perish, but have everlasting life" (John 3:16).

"Beloved, let us love one another: for love is of God; and every one that loves is born of God, and knows God. He that loves not knows not God; for God is love (I John 4: 7-8).

"And we have known and believed the love that God hath to us. God is love; and he that dwells in love dwells in God, and God in him" (I John 4:16).

"There is no fear in love, but perfect love casts out fear: because fear hath torment. He that fears is not made perfect in love" (I John 4:18).

"The Lord hath appeared of old unto me, saying, Yea, I have loved thee with an everlasting love; therefore with loving kindness have I drawn thee." (Jeremiah 31:3).

Just like we have to eat food to feed our body. We must take in God's word to feed our spirit. When our spirit is weak, we are unable to handle certain things in life. Not getting the word can make us spiritually weak, so we are not able to handle the spiritual fight when it comes.

As you read God's word and spend time with him in prayer you are becoming strong. You are more aware of your environment. You are aware of your influence on the people around you as well as their influence on you. You start noticing things that you didn't notice before from your new perspective. The earth is the Lord's and the fullness thereof..... (Psalm 24:1). You are aware that you were created for a reason. You are aware that the enemy doesn't want you to have your new found peace. You feel as if you are living in another time zone, you see everything in a different light. It's different but you know you are on the right path. You also notice how the old path is so near that you can jump back on it, but you don't want that. You feel yourself changing in many different ways. You now notice what you never noticed before. Your responses to others are different. When you spend time with God first, it governs the rest of your day. His influence touches all of your life. Make time to spend with God alone with no distractions no cell phone, television or anything else. The time you spend with him in fellowship can multiply your position in other areas of your life in the most positive ways.

C. Church-The Good, The Bad, The Ugly

The church is a very interesting! I paused to include it in this book but I must. This book is for you. It's not about my feelings. Many people have opinions on the church that cause them to either attend or not attend. Church has more than one definition. The context in which I describe it now is related to the physical space and people that come together to meet weekly. We blame the church for so many issues of which it could never be fully responsible. Let me explain to you about the church from the perspective of paradoxes. Paradoxes consider two sides of an argument. The church is good because it gives you an opportunity to spend some time with other believers. On the contrary, everyone in the church doesn't believe the same thing. The church is filled with some wonderful people, on the contrary the church has some people that may not be so wonderful. The church shows love, on the contrary, the church can also show you the ugliest side of hate. The church is where we join together and praise God, on the contrary the church can divide us. There is no perfect church. Even before you consider church, your first priority is spending time in God's word and in prayer. God wants to communicate with you on a daily basis. He doesn't want you just opening the pages of the bible on the day you attend church. His word is more valuable than that and it deserves daily attention. One of the greatest purposes for attending church is to hear from God. Yes, God can speak to us anytime He wants to, but He also has someone to minister to us as well. As you decide on a church you would like to attend, pray about this and pay attention. I was led to my current church when I heard music coming out of the back of a vehicle. My kids and I were coming out of the movie theatre. I had not been to church in a while due to physical illness. But I definitely needed a church home at that time but had only stopped to inquire about the music and was invited to attend the church. I have been in love with my church since then. It is so important to me and my family. There are many different ministers and many different churches. You should find one where you feel love and you are able to "hear" the minister. It doesn't mean that everyone will show you love, but feeling love means the presence of God is there. Again no church is perfect, no minister is perfect, we are not perfect, but we must find our best place for growth. If someone has decided not to attend church because of the people, they will never attend church. There will always be people there, all of whom are imperfect. You have to make a decision that you want to hear from God. While you may not connect with everyone there, that's okay. If you find one or two people with whom you can connect great. Be an example of being the best you that you are, don't be concerned about what other people are not. Everyone in church is not on the same level, everyone has potential for growth. Everyone in church is not interested in growing. Some people are there to be obstacles, you can't worry about them, and you must focus on what you need. You do have the responsibility to visit different churches to find one that will work for you and what you need. God's word tells us to come together as a body (Hebrews 25) "Not forsaking the assembling of ourselves together...." So if He says it, it is true. It is prideful to say you don't need something that God says you do. As you grow more spiritually, you will notice that your study of the word and your prayer life and the pastor's message will coincide for you in some way. You will grow spiritually. There can be many people in church that feel the pastor is talking directly to their situation and he is. The Holy Spirit is one and the same. The same Holy Spirit that will speak to you and show you things, is the same Holy Spirit that speaks to your pastor. So when you go to church you should go with expectation to hear the word. It may not be what you want to hear but it will always be what you need to grow. Love your church, support your church and respect your pastor.

The other definition of church is the part of you that praises God, reads God's word and communes with God all by yourself. This church lives inside of you, it is with you all the time. Be wary of those who say "the church is in me, I don't need to attend church". Sorry but this again is prideful it says "I don't need anybody else, I don't want to be around anybody else". We all need other people, if we didn't we'd have our own personal planets. People will also deny needing a church because they don't want to help support the church financially. It's like saying I want the benefits of living in a home but I don't want to help pay the bills. The church has expenses and depends on its members to pay tithes and offerings. While there may be good and bad churches, this is no reason not to support the church of which you are a member. And remember you freely choose which church you want to join. You need your church and your church needs you. Paying tithes also brings you into covenant with God regarding your finances Malachi 3:10.

You are your Second Love

Now that you understand why God is your first love, it should be easy to understand how you must be your second love. So the world's view that "You come first" is flawed. "You come second, only after God". Now please don't let pride get in the way. Some would think "how would I not be first?" But if you think about it, without God, you wouldn't exist anyway. He created us and He made the rules. It's as simple as that. No one has a different arrangement, it's the same for us all. It's actually because of God, who is love, that we even first begin to comprehend what love is. Our creator always deserves our honor, our reverence and our respect. It is only after we revere Him, are we able to even know how to love.   If I have love for myself without God, that's just pride. If I think I am more than I really am, eventually I will let myself down because I am not a creator and I have no power without God.

Many people work by their own efforts. Our own efforts can get us so far. There are millionaires and billionaires with wealth but no peace, no love or no joy. God wants us to have a relationship with Him. Then by virtue of that relationship, the wealth comes.

What does it mean to love yourself? You have concern for your mental/spiritual, physical, and financial health. Life is a juggle of activities. As women, we can have so many responsibilities. We are employees, business owners, wives, daughters, sisters, mothers, friends, co-workers, cooks, maids, church members, relatives, etc. We have so many titles and roles. We have many people that depend on us for one reason or another. Physically as women, we are special. Our bodies are complicated and require our attention. We have to maintain our health and our appearance. That is a job within itself. This book is focused on some of our mental/spiritual needs. Also, with our financial health, we must know what finances are needed for our lives. We must understand what our income is, our financial obligations and our expenses. We must budget well. In loving ourselves we must consider each of these areas. If we love ourselves, we value ourselves. If we value ourselves, we won't allow others just to treat us any kind of way. After we learn to love God first then ourselves, only then can we love others. The bible teaches us to ".....Thou shalt love thy neighbor as thyself." Mark 12:31 which means that we must first know how to love ourselves. We love ourselves by honoring ourselves. We honor ourselves by monitoring our mental/spiritual, physical and financial needs. Our mental and spiritual are connected because we must first realize and understand who we are. And our thinking must line up with the word of God. We must capture our idle thoughts that don't agree with God's word. As women, we can think faster than light travels. Depending on how we allow our mind to wander, we can go from happy to sad in seconds. We have to watch and monitor our own self-talk inside of our heads. Proverbs 18:21 speaks of the power of life and death are in the tongue. It's easy for us to say something or think something negative about yourself. It's harder to think the best sometimes. So we have to decide whether to believe our automatic negative thoughts or to believe God's word. There are many scriptures that talk about God's love for us and that are inspirational and feed our mind and spirit. You have to choose if you are going to believe God's word or the enemy's. Studying and focusing on God's words daily can change your mind, which changes your language, which changes your conversation and which will change your reality. Romans 12:2 "And be not conformed to this world: but be ye transformed by the renewing of your mind, that ye may prove what is that good, and acceptable, and perfect, will of God". Take some of the most inspirational scriptures for yourself and focus on them daily. Say them daily as many times as you need to, to get them into your spirit. Write them down and put them in places you spend time. Your life depends on your reliance and belief and trust in God's word. You can also find scriptures that will encourage you in different situations. For the purpose of this book, leaving a relationship that you wanted to work but didn't can cause frustration, shame and loneliness. Some encouraging scriptures are:

"He healeth the broken in heart, and bindeth up their wounds." Psalm 147:3

 "For the Lord will not forsake his people for his great name's sake: because it hath pleased the Lord to make you His people." I Samuel 12:22

"Fear thou not; for I am with thee: be not dismayed for I am thy God: I will strengthen thee; yea I will help thee: yea, I will uphold thee with the right hand of my righteousness" Isaiah 41:10

"….I will never leave thee nor forsake thee." Hebrews 13:5

"Casting all your care upon him; for he careth for you." I Peter 5:7

"God is our refuge and strength, a very present help in trouble." Psalm 46:1

"For His anger endureth but a moment; in his favor is life; weeping may endure for a night, but joy cometh in the morning." Psalm 30:5

"For I am persuaded, that neither death, nor life, nor angels, nor principalities, nor powers, nor things present, nor things to come, nor height, nor depth, nor any other creature, shall be able to separate us from the love of God, which is in Christ Jesus our Lord." Romans 8: 38,39

Find the scriptures that speak to you, while all scripture is for us, there are some that speak to us more soundly and clearly than others. Focus on these scriptures, for some reason these are the scriptures where your faith in God is stronger. Stand on them.

As women we need help, we can't do it all on our own. When I was started my business, I made a list of things I had to do. Some tasks were simple and easy, others were so complicated for me, I almost wanted to quit. One task in particular that made me feel this way was completing my website. I was given instruction on how to start it and how to see which options I wanted it to have etc. It was fun at first, but then there were some things that would not work for me and I became frustrated to the point of stopping everything. I finally contacted my friend who is an expert at this and asked for her help. I would pay her anything to take this burden from me. I met with her the next day and the website was completed. I was so happy and felt so much better. It was like a huge burden or boulder had been taken off my shoulders. Only then was I able to press on and tackle other tasks that I was capable of, like writing this book for you. So ladies, when you need help get it. We weren't made to solve our every problem. In the multitude of counselors there is safety (Proverbs 24:6) the bible teaches us many times that we need help. Whatever help you need get it. Whether it be physical help, go to the physician, the medical specialist, read God's word on healing get what you need. Whether it be mental/spiritual see your pastor, church ministry, a Christian counselor, read God's word, read a book or find resources on the internet whatever you need. When there is a fee for a service, pay it, these people are trained to help you and are worthy of their labor. (I Timothy 5:18) If you need financial help see a CPA, financial planner, read God's word on finances. I tell you that it is such a relief when you can lean on others and not have to be fully self-sufficient. God did not intend for us to go it alone anyway. God's people have purposes and reasons for existing and they always focus on helping others. So as you are getting the help, find out also to whom you can be helpful. We need each other.

Do you really want to leave the relationship?

Okay, back to what's going on with Joe. You notice that when you spend time with God, it doesn't even bother you that Joe isn't calling as much. What's changed? You have. You are beginning to realize that Joe is not your source of strength God is. As you are coming away from this relationship that is not healthy for you, there will be situations that will arise to try and draw you back. You will go through some days where you may want the relationship back.

Joe will call or text more now, because you are no longer complaining about not hearing from him enough or spending time with him. One thing about Joe, for some strange reason, it makes him feel good when you get angry or upset with him for not calling or spending enough time with you. Not sure why, but the anger means you care, he's got you hooked or his work in truly "getting you" is done. I don't understand his part, but I do yours. In times past, you would think about Joe, now Joe is thinking about you. He is wondering what you are up to. Why are you not bothering him about spending more time with you? Am I saying that Joe can't change? No, but my concern is still with you, keep growing your relationship with God.

It's just like a diet, when you have to keep going to see the true results and reach your goals. Keep God first, even if you are still in the relationship with Joe. Your relationship with God won't change Joe and it's not supposed to, but it will change you. In time, whether Joe calls or not it won't bother you at all. You will begin to judge Joe based upon his own words AND corresponding action. "Hey babe, I gotta go, I'll call you back later tonight". If the call doesn't come you will notice that, but it won't surprise you and it won't hurt you. Now if Joe is not crazy and abusive you can stay in a relationship in a limited manner and learn something. If it's abusive and dangerous get out and get personal, legal and any professional help you need right now.   If you want to break up with him you can do that if you need that type of directness. Or you can just let the relationship slide down the drain like a flat soda. If you decide to just stay in the relationship and keep growing closer to

God, you will see things you never saw before. The rose tinted love glasses will become crystal clear.

If you feel yourself thinking about Joe and it's not constructive and you don't want to think about him, think about Jesus. Quote some of your favorite scriptures for such times as these. (God will keep you in perfect peace whose mind is stayed on Him, Isaiah 26:3) or whatever you have a need for that is more important to you than Joe. Don't let Joe rent space in your mind, when he can't even keep a promise to call you back.

If you decide to break up with Joe because he doesn't give you what you need, remember that was the original problem. You are really breaking up with Joe now because you deserve much better. To tell him that now, would be mean, because you had accepted him on different terms. You may want to tell him that your life is going in a different direction and that you wish him well. Now regardless of what you say, he will think that you have met someone else. He will feel that you have rejected him. Now again, I don't know why Joe thinks that but he does. And really you have met someone new, God. So you really have been cheating on Joe with God. If Joe is just a good guy, he won't really understand. So it's up to you to tell him what you want to tell him. But part of the great beauty of being a woman is that we can always change our mind, what we wanted yesterday we don't want it anymore. What is really true about that statement is not that men can't change their minds, but nobody can communicate their change of mind like a woman. Regardless of what you do, how you do it, be safe and don't complicate things further.

Your connection with God will change everything

While your relationship with God is on the increase and your relationship with Joe is on the decrease, other relationships in your life will be affected. If you have friends and tell them about what's been going on, they may not see things your way. That's fine. A true friend will honor your growth and encourage you to keep getting closer to God. If they don't condone your new relationship with God, you must consider that this relationship may have to go as well. Sometimes friends take time to adjust, so you decide if the friendship is worth giving that time. Your lifestyle may have changed because of your relationship with God. You may no longer do some of the things you used to do such as cursing, going out to clubs and a variety of other activities with a long list. If your friends are connected to you by these activities they will feel neglected by you. They may feel that you are changing. They may think that you think you are better than they are. They may feel intimidated that you will judge them for not changing at the same pace you did. They may not have a desire to change. They may even start seeing Joe. Or you may find out they were already seeing Joe behind your back anyway. Remember this is not to say that as you grow your relationship with God you will stop doing everything that was fun. That's not true. Many have a perception of what your life should look like if you are living to please God that is based on myth, prejudices, and downright lies. So you will have decisions to make about these other relationships in your life. Here is another area where you can ask God to help you make major decisions. Sometimes people will make the decision for you and leave on their own. You will miss them, but what you will gain from your relationship with God is more valuable than anything else. He can give you the right friendships. But remember let no one or nothing separate you from God. If you guard that relationship, God will guard you in area arena of your life. You will become stronger. What you couldn't handle before you will now master.

The Greatest Discovery in Spending Time with God

There is one remarkable thing that occurs when you start spending time with God. You discover how much He loves you. You discover that it has nothing to do with you personally. His love is not based upon your behavior or your words. He loves you because He is love. You learn that God has plans for his creation. He created you for purpose and with great intention. You realize you didn't get here by yourself. You realize how dependent on Him you really are, for every breath you breathe. In discovering this love of God, you start to see yourself as He sees you. Your self- esteem increases. God loves you just the way you are. He is there when you sleep, and when you awake. He enjoys spending time with you. He brings peace and love every time you show up to spend time with Him. He looks forward to you spending time with Him. He's never too busy for you. You may have forgotten Him, but He never forgets you. He loved and knew you before you were formed in your mother's womb. He gave His son for you so that you could live with Him forever. He is ever present. He never lies. He never makes promises He doesn't keep. He would be the perfect man, but He's not a man, He is our father.

You now are in a relationship with someone who has given you an open door for communication. While, you still may be learning how to listen and hear from God. His word is speaking to your spirit now. You are praying and asking for guidance and help. If you continue seeking, the help will surely come, the sweet Holy Spirit. He leads us into all truth. He answers our questions. He tells us things that He hears from the Father. Everything He tells us is for our life and how to live and what's to come. What the sweet Holy Spirit imparts to us is wisdom, He gives us a living right now word for our situation in life. At this time, you start asking Him things. "What does God want me to do?" "For what purpose was I created?" "How do I leave this relationship?" "I'm confused what is really going on in this relationship?" The Holy Spirit speaks in peaceful times, but He can speak anytime He wants. I have been in the middle of something and His word comes to me so clear and peacefully. It wasn't audible, not to say that it can't be. We can never try to put the Holy Spirit in a box. He is God, He can do whatever He wants and how He wants. But make sure you have times of peace with no outside distractions. You won't always like what you hear, but that doesn't matter. It's not about your feelings it's about truth and getting wisdom.

Update: the relationship

Okay, now you are seeing things differently? Things that you might have neglected paying attention to before are getting your full attention now. You call Joe and get no answer. It hurts, but just let it hurt. It will stop eventually. Keep spending that one on one time with God, reading His word and praying. Remember He is always there and He wants and desires to spend time with you. You will begin to notice that it doesn't hurt as much when you don't hear from Joe or even if he doesn't text or whatever. You begin to think, "I am a wonderful woman, I'm God's child, and how dare Joe not see how wonderful I am" so eventually you will come to the conclusion that Joe is stupid or slow on the uptake. Now you still care about Joe, you still miss Joe, but your mind is changing about who YOU are. Eventually you will reach out less to Joe, because you have come to realize that you deserve more. When Joe does come by or invites you over. You unknowingly start judging his words by God's word. May I say, fortunately Joe doesn't have a chance. Joe may ask you these questions because you are not sweating him like you were before. "What have you been up to?" Even though he doesn't tell you what he's been up to, as a matter of fact, his conversation is very superficial and shallow. He never talked about anything important that was going on in his life and definitely spoke nothing about your relationship with him. Having sex with Joe now, will be different. You now know you need and deserve more than what he is offering. You don't feel as connected to him as you did before. Sex may not even be enjoyable now with Joe. As you get closer to God, you start to value what He values. God values you. You start to see your life how God sees your life. Your life and body belong to God. Your body is a temple and is precious. "Give not that which is holy unto the dogs, neither cast ye your pearls before swine...... (Matthew 7:6)" Okay I'm not calling Joe a dog or a pig, but he is unworthy and I didn't write the Bible.

You are beautiful, precious, created with purpose, created on purpose, loved unconditionally, you look like your Father because He made you in His image, He has great plans for your life, He loves spending time with you, He loves that you read and honor His word, He loves that you seek Him first. He wants the best for you. If Joe isn't good to you, for you, he doesn't realize how valuable you are, doesn't honor your Father by respecting His daughter (you). Joe is not God's best for you. You don't need Joe. In time, you won't want Joe.   "What I need (to be emotionally healthy) is now far more important than what I thought I wanted". T. Phillips, 2014.

It won't be easy, but if you keep going. You will win. The smaller goal is to come out of this relationship with Joe.

The Greatest Goal (Matthew 6:33)

The greatest goal is to enter a relationship with your heavenly Father. Once you enter this new, greatest, best relationship with God it will help you govern every other relationship in your life. You won't allow someone like Joe to get that close to you again. You will begin seeing things you never saw before. The sweet Holy Spirit will speak to you about people when you ask Him. You will now have a wealth of wisdom that will assist you in pursuing anything in your life. Although we as women put a lot of stock in being in a relationship with a man, it isn't the most important thing in life. It's not even close. The most important thing in our life is honoring and serving our heavenly Father. Living by His word that never fails. Finding out why He created us and pursuing that as our life's goal. Loving others as we love ourselves. When it's time for a new relationship, it will be time for a new relationship. Forget about what the world says or how they view you, you get your identity from God. He will never lead you wrong. He is always faithful. Enjoy getting closer with Him. Whatever relationship you get into next with a man, will be judged based upon how well He knows your father. You will hold them to that standard. If daddy says no, it will never be right. We think we know what we want, but I believe God knows what we want and need far better than we do. He knows me better than I will ever know myself. He created me. He knows every cell in my body and every hair on my head. He knows my tomorrows today. He knows my ending from the beginning. Allow Him to have some say so to whoever you allow to get close to you. Not just romantic relationships, but with any relationship allow God to guide you and speak into those situations. When the Holy Spirit speaks to you it will always line up with the word of God, it will never oppose it for He is God.

If you love God, He will teach you how to love someone else. You can and will fall sometimes, ask for forgiveness and get back up its okay.   God still loves you and has plans for your life.

Conclusion: The Revelations

*What Joe does or does not do, has nothing to do with who you are.

*Joe doesn't determine your worth, you and God do.

*Once you know your worth, you won't have to wait or look for someone else to validate it.

*Remember it's really not about your feelings. So stop feeling bad when Joe doesn't "act right" or the way you think he should.

*Joe can't "act right" because he's not supposed to "act right". He may be a good guy but you're a great woman. Good doesn't deserve great. Good wants great, that's why he's lurking around in the first place. But why should great (you) settle for good (him)?

*God's word is true all the time, it has nothing to do with Joe or your feelings.

This book was meant to be short, it's a guide not a novel. "….Write the vision and make it plain upon tables, that he (she) may run that readeth it" (Habakkuk 2:2)

Run, you are a winner. God loves you and so do I.

Sincerely,

Tara

www.taraphillipsconsulting.com

Tara Phillips Consulting LLC

Email: taraphillips.consulting@gmail.com

www.ingramcontent.com/pod-product-compliance
Lightning Source LLC
Chambersburg PA
CBHW051434090426
42737CB00014B/2974